On the Elevator

Add and Subtract Within 20

Tom Rosado

INFOMAX
COMMON CORE MATH
READERS

Rosen
Classroom™

New York

Published in 2014 by The Rosen Publishing Group, Inc.
29 East 21st Street, New York, NY 10010

Book Design: Jon D'Rozario

Photo Credits: Cover JJ Studio/Shutterstock.com; p. 5 Inhabitant/Shutterstock.com; pp. 7, 9, 11, 13, 15, 17, 19, 21
(buttons) kontur-vid/Shutterstock.com; pp. 7, 9, 11, 13, 15, 17, 19, 21(background) Claudio Divizia/Shutterstock.com;
pp. 9, 13 (boy) Monkey Business Images/Shutterstock.com; pp. 11, 13 (girl) Nico Traut/Shutterstock.com; p. 15 Sklep
Spozywczy/Shutterstock.com; p. 17 Dragon Images/Shutterstock.com; p. 19 Yuri Arcurs/Shutterstock.com;
p. 21 Jupiterimages/ThinkStock.com; p. 22 hxdbzxy/Shuttestock.com.

ISBN: 978-1-4777-2124-7
6-pack ISBN: 978-1-4777-2125-4

Manufactured in the United States of America

CPSIA Compliance Information: Batch #CS13RC: For further information contact Rosen Publishing, New York, New York at 1-800-237-9932.

Word Count: 311

Contents

A Tall Building

My family lives in a tall building. It has 20 floors! We live on the top floor. We use an **elevator** to go up and down in our building.

I like to push the buttons on the elevator. Since our building has 20 floors, there are 20 buttons. I count 2 rows with 10 buttons each.

(19) (20)

(17) (18)

(15) (16)

(13) (14)

(11) (12)

(9) (10)

(7) (8)

(5) (6)

(3) (4)

(1) (2)

Seeing My Friends

My friend Dan lives on floor 14. I get in the elevator to go see him. I count the floors as the elevator goes down. I count 6 floors from 20 to 14.

$$20 - 6 = 14$$

Dan and I want to play with our friend Megan. She lives on floor 8. Since we're starting on floor 14, we have to go down 6 more floors.

$$14 - 6 = 8$$

There are 6 floors from my floor to Dan's. There are 6 floors from Dan's floor to Megan's. When I add 6 and 6, I get 12. That means I traveled down 12 floors.

6 + 6 = 12

Going Outside

My friends and I want to go play outside. We need to take the elevator to floor 1. If we're on floor 8, how many floors will we go down?

$$8 - 1 = 7$$

We play outside for a long time. Then, I have to go home. Many people ride the elevator up with me. Mr. Lopez needs to get off at floor 11. I count 10 floors as the elevator goes up.

1 + 10 = 11

Mrs. Cater tells me she's going to floor 16. I know that 11 and 5 make 16. That means the elevator will go up 5 floors before she gets off.

11 + 5 = 16

My floor isn't too far away. I know that 16 and 4 make 20. I also know that if I take 16 from 20, I have 4. Now I know that I only have to go up 4 floors.

16 + 4 = 20

20 - 16 = 4

Lots of Fun

Riding the elevator is a lot of fun! I like to push the buttons. Is there an elevator where you live?

Glossary

elevator (EH-luh-vay-tuhr) A moving room with doors that carries people up and down in a building.

Index